D1716956

SATURN

by Ariel Kazunas

CHERRY LAKE PUBLISHING * ANN ARBOR, MICHIGAN

Published in the United States of America by Cherry Lake Publishing
Ann Arbor, Michigan
www.cherrylakepublishing.com

Content Adviser: Dr. Tobias Owen, University of Hawaii Institute for Astronomy

Photo Credits: Cover, ©Orlando Florin Rosu/Dreamstime.com; cover and pages 10, 12, 14, 16, 18, and 20, ©NASA; page 4, ©ASSOCIATED PRESS/EUROPEAN SPACE AGENCY ESA; page 6, ©Orla/Shutterstock, Inc.; page 8, ©ASSOCIATED PRESS

LIBRARY OF CONGRESS CATALOGING-IN-PUBLICATION DATA
Kazunas, Ariel.
  Saturn/by Ariel Kazunas.
      p. cm.—(21st century junior library)
  Includes bibliographical references and index.
  ISBN-13: 978-1-61080-087-7 (lib. bdg.)
  ISBN-10: 1-61080-087-7 (lib. bdg.)
  1. Saturn (Planet)—Juvenile literature. I. Title.
  QB671.K25 2011
  523.46—dc22   2010052609

*Cherry Lake Publishing would like to acknowledge the work of
The Partnership for 21st Century Skills.
Please visit* www.21stcenturyskills.org *for more information.*

Printed in the United States of America
Corporate Graphics Inc.
July 2011
CLFA09

CONTENTS

5 Spectacular Saturn

9 Huge but Not Heavy

13 Rocky Rings

17 Many Moons

22 Glossary

23 Find Out More

24 Index

24 About the Author

Saturn's rings make it easy to recognize.

Spectacular Saturn

Saturn is one of the most beautiful planets in our **solar system**. It is known for its yellow color and wide rings.

Saturn is the sixth planet from the Sun. It is the farthest planet from Earth that can be easily seen without a **telescope**.

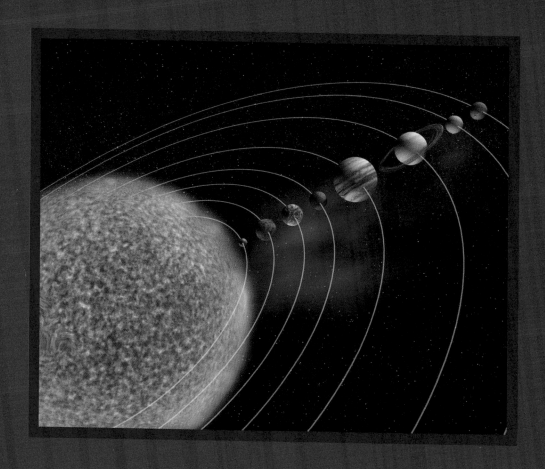

Planets that are farther from the Sun have
longer years.

There are eight planets in our solar system. They all travel around the Sun. The time it takes for a planet to **orbit** the Sun one time is called a year.

Saturn takes a long time to orbit the Sun. This is because it is so far away. One year on Saturn is almost as long as 30 years on Earth.

Look! Try looking for Saturn in the night sky. Your teacher or librarian can help you look up how to find it.

Saturn is very large, but it is only a little more than half the size of Jupiter.

Huge but Not Heavy

Saturn is one of the biggest planets in our solar system. Only Jupiter is bigger. Earth could fit inside Saturn 766 times!

Create!

You can use fruit to see just how big Saturn is. Pretend Earth is the size of a blueberry. Saturn would be as big as a coconut!

The four biggest planets in our solar system are made of gas.

A planet so big seems like it would be very heavy. But Saturn is very light. This is because it is made mostly of gases. Scientists think these gases probably swirl around a solid **core**.

Saturn's rings are made of millions of tiny pieces
of rock and ice.

Rocky Rings

An object in space was destroyed near Saturn long ago. Saturn's **gravity** pulled in the broken pieces of rock and ice. These pieces formed rings around the planet.

Saturn has three main rings. There are also many smaller ones.

Saturn's rings look thinner from the side.

Jupiter, Uranus, and Neptune also have rings. Saturn's are the largest. They only look big from above. All you can see from the side is a thin line around the planet.

Ask Questions!

Spacecraft give scientists information about Saturn. Four spacecraft have visited Saturn since 1979. Ask a teacher or librarian to help you learn more about them.

Saturn's moons are many different sizes.

Many Moons

More than 60 moons orbit Saturn. They are all different. Some have icy mountains. Others are covered with **craters**. One moon is even shaped like a can of soup!

Titan's atmosphere is full of clouds.

Saturn's biggest moon is called Titan. A Dutch scientist discovered it in 1655 by looking through a telescope.

Titan is bigger than the planet Mercury. It is the only moon in our solar system with a cloudy **atmosphere** like Earth's. But unlike Earth, Titan's clouds are not made of water. Titan is also the only known object other than Earth to have liquid on its surface.

Titan could provide important clues about how life started on Earth.

Titan's atmosphere is a lot like Earth's was a long time ago. This means studying Titan might help us discover how life started on Earth.

There is still a lot to learn about Saturn and its moons. What will we learn next?

Make a Guess!

Why do you think scientists want to study Titan? Remember that Titan might give scientists clues about how life first began on Earth. How could this information be useful to scientists?

GLOSSARY

atmosphere (AT-muhss-fihr) the gases or air surrounding a planet

core (KOR) center part of a planet

craters (KRAY-turz) holes caused by one object in space hitting another

gravity (GRAV-uh-tee) the invisible force between objects in space that makes them pull on each other

orbit (OR-bit) to travel in a path around a central point

solar system (SOH-lur SISS-tuhm) a star, such as the Sun, and all the planets and moons that move around it

telescope (TEL-uh-skohp) a tool used to look at faraway objects

FIND OUT MORE

BOOKS

Aguilar, David A. *11 Planets: A New View of the Solar System*. Washington, DC: National Geographic Society, 2008.

Landau, Elaine. *Saturn*. New York: Children's Press, 2008.

Waxman, Laura Hamilton. *Saturn*. Minneapolis: Lerner Publications, 2010.

WEB SITES

HubbleSite Gallery
hubblesite.org/gallery
Take a look at some cool pictures of outer space.

NASA: Solar System Exploration
solarsystem.nasa.gov/kids
Check out these fun activities from NASA.

Space.com—Our Solar System: Facts, Formation and Discovery
www.space.com/solarsystem/
Learn more about the objects in our solar system and how they were formed.

INDEX

A
atmosphere, 19, 21

C
color, 5
core, 11
craters, 17

G
gases, 11
gravity, 13

J
Jupiter, 9, 15

L
location, 5, 7

M
moons, 17, 19, 21

N
Neptune, 15

O
orbit, 7, 17

R
rings, 5, 13, 15

S
scientists, 11, 15, 21
size, 9
solar system, 5, 7, 9, 19

S
spacecraft, 15
Sun, 5, 7

T
telescopes, 5
Titan (moon), 19, 21

U
Uranus, 15

W
weight, 11

Y
years, 7

ABOUT THE AUTHOR

Ariel Kazunas lives on the Oregon coast, writing books for kids and working at the Sitka Center for Art and Ecology. She has also worked for several nonprofit magazines. Ariel loves exploring our planet, Earth—especially by hand, foot, bike, and boat—and camping out under the stars.